Over and Over

Poems

By Samantha Schwind

Table of Contents

The world offers itself to your imagination,
calls to you like the wild geese, harsh and exciting -
over and over announcing your place
in the family of things.

~Mary Oliver, "Wild Geese"

Spoken Word

This Is What Unrequited Love Feels Like

My heart was a second-story window
and you jumped out anyway

so I made my heart into a trampoline
where we jumped
laughing in midair
but you couldn't stay still

and my heart became a promise
that I couldn't seem to keep

because my heart was a sandcastle
and you were the approaching tide

so I squeezed my heart into a diamond
and you became the most precious jewel thief

I tried to be more careful
so I crafted my heart into a wishing well
but you were penniless
and I wanted to give you everything I had

so I built my heart into a cabin in the woods
and you walked right in

and my heart became a candle
that you lit up
and melted

and then I built my heart into a lighthouse
and I brought you home

and my heart flowed into a waterfall
cascading
thundering
flowing
but you couldn't swim

so my heart became a ship
lost in a stormy sea
and you were the lightning above
We could no longer touch
for fear of ultimate destruction
but I needed you to see me

so I made my heart a mirror
and you looked right through it

so I turned my heart into a bridge
that I thought could connect me to you
but you wouldn't meet me halfway

because my heart is a tarot deck
and you are the hanging man
always, the hanging man

so I threw my heart against the wall
and it bounced back as a lemon
which I pressed into your hand
and screamed *Make of it what you will!*
You called me bitter
but I still wanted to nourish you

so I folded my heart into
a CrunchWrap Supreme
but of course you gave up meat

so my heart became an egg
cracked over an open flame
but you left before breakfast

and then my heart was a secret
that you couldn't seem to keep

and my heart played on as a gramophone
but you were every song
every skipping record
every tune stuck in my head

so I wrote my heart down in a book
but you preferred to read the skies

so my heart exploded into a star
and I said *Make a wish*
but your head was in the clouds

so my heart became a bird
sometimes singing
sometimes soaring
sometimes scrounging
for breadcrumbs.

My heart has lived so many lives
over and over
that I almost forgot to ask:

What is your heart?

Radio Silence

I don't believe the world will end
in fire, nor ice, nor some cataclysmic
nuclear device. No; I'm pretty sure
the end of the world will arrive
in a mess of unanswered texts.

Trust me, I would know best,
though I wish I knew better
after receiving so many ghosts
in place of love letters.

The sense of doom that comes
from a sent message with no reply is
unparalleled in its passive panic, just
radio silence where there would have been
static, could have been music, should
have been at least a pathetic

"Let's get together another day" or even
a polite "Nah, but thanks anyway,"
but no way, just another
fizzled-out fade-away.

Radio silence, no tangible message,
just a subtle hint indicating lack
of interest. The quiet,
a commonality of this modern century,

stems from a lack of courtesy
I can't begin to fathom.

Would it be too forward to want
something more, to stop feeling ignored?

The unanswered text presents
a mystery, frustrating in its ambiguity.
This unique type of let-down, devoid
of closure, makes me lose my composure
and avoids any reciprocation
once the recipient
cuts the line of communication.

I can't stand to be forgotten, it's like
they put no thought into just how
this would play out. I could shout
for thirty days about this murky haze
of muted discourse, but of course
even a month's worth of sulking
just adds up to nothing.

It can be tense and perhaps best
to pretend when the silence is loaded,
so I type out a peace-out to clarify
my ambivalence finally:
"Tens don't get ghosted, so
I'm assuming you died.
R.I.P."

Payphone Prayer

My connection with God
is a long-distance call.

Every night, the stars shimmer
through my bedroom window as I lay
down on my worn-out pillow.

Thoughts from the day
swim through the air,
fears and cares and hopes I can't share,
until I turn off the lights
and clasp my hands in prayer.

A thin silver thread
extends from the moon to my bed,
telephone wires exploding in my head
that inspire a spiritual dialogue to
transpire—

I recite the words I learned
when I was young, cadence
of innocence leaving my tongue
as my heart beats in time
with long-ago-learned
Sunday school lines.

Our Father, who art
in heaven, hallowed
be thy name…

The words are familiar, always the same,
but for some reason, over the years,
they've changed.

What I once saw as poetry
has now become perfunctory,
with the beauty of divinity
shrouded in uncertainty. Still,
they're a part of my nightly routine –

I feel at home in these lines,
like knowing your own area code
after calling home so many times.

Not exactly a sacred remembrance,
but not forgetting bears naked semblance
to "keeping the faith"—
it's commonplace
to stick with what you know.

Even as doubts grow,
it's hard to let go
of what soothed you as truth
so long ago.

O God, renew a
steadfast spirit
within me…

So flawed, I can't hear it clearly.
Sleeping with a brass cross beneath my head
for so long seems to have prolonged
a crick in my neck and a trip in my step.

The conversation starts to lag,
and I know I'm holding back—
this little piece of universe
that I can't quite reach starts to blur
with the hopes and desires that defer
my sleep, unseen telephone wires
encircling me.

God, grant me the serenity
to accept the things
I cannot change…

I wish the exchange
could last longer, but I
don't have enough change,
just a heart that wants to be
stronger but starts to blow apart
whenever I consider how I
no longer feel what I did as a kid.

Back then, I was certain,
never questioned a sermon—
Every good story starts out optimistically,
the short version being as a child I had no fears
because God was in my ears,
not light-years away.

Now I've got beliefs that won't stay,
and phone bills to pay (of the
metaphysical sort, of course,
because how can I call collect
if I can't suspect
a mighty being in the distance
might be listening?)

Tomorrow night I'll try again,
hoping someone is
around to pick up the phone as I lay down
my faith with my sleeping form
and say goodnight with a soft

Amen.

Untitled Space Poem

for Urfa, even now

Tonight I can feel the distance between us,
the miles that I wear around my neck like a scarf.

Even with the loops and loops of a loose
connection, I stand shivering in a cold wind
that demands to be felt, to be noticed,
and the wind always wins.

The space between us
is constantly shifting and stretching,
contracting and compressing,
elongating and enveloping,
ever-present and insistent.

This precious invisible
abyss becomes the sundial by which
I mark my days, swaying with me
like a shadow.

This distance,
the thousands of silent
footsteps between a door
and a conversation—

The same feeling I had the other day
when I was driving

and suddenly a small green spider
crept across the windshield directly
before my line of vision

and in this moment
the spider and I
existed alone together,

outside of time
in the same suspended space,
essentially motionless yet
speeding along,
hanging in the balance,

acknowledging
the gap between us
but staring straight ahead
and moving forward.

See, these poems spill
into existence, and I pretend like
the bizarre incidence of our
inadvertent congruence can be
written out and studied, like a
treasure map of my own heart

and I am silly to think of space like a scarf,
which reminds me that there is nothing
to know but fresh air and deep breath and room to grow.

This space spins memories into
night sky constellations,
solid as stories, sturdy as sighs.

This space holds
the outline of a home
with high ceilings
and open windows and
promises just big enough
to break.

When the music dies

down and all the clocks stop,
this distance between us
is how I keep time in the silent
opera house of my own mind.

This space is the place where I
will see you over and over
and say "Thank you
for meeting me
here."

Love Letters

Love Letter from the House Plant to the Tea Kettle

They told me
that I was meant for a life in the shade,
a seat by the clearest window, and that you
would just hang me up
to leave me high and dry.

They said
that I was too young, far too
green for love, and that you
would just burn up
the seeds of my blossoming
potential.

They told me
that I would always be turning toward
your chromium charm just to hear you whistle
after some porcelain model, and that you
were filled with far too much
hot air
for someone as
calm, cool, and collected
as me.

They told me
that you were nothing more
than a dream,
insubstantial as steam.

But I
know you,
I've seen you, and I
have a feeling deep
in my roots about you.

I have seen past
your shiny, stainless-steel armor,
and I have felt
your calm inner warmth.

I will let you make tea
and cool down with me
in peace
whenever you please.

If loving you
means getting steamy, bring on
the fire, I will leave this windowsill behind
in pursuit of desire. I'm accustomed
to weekly waterings, but with you, I'll take
whatever you're willing to give.

And I know
we live in different worlds,
and we're both always
really busy,
but in my dreams,
when we face each other,

it is so bright that I
wake up feeling like
sunlight – so,
maybe one day, you'll
leave your fiery hotspot to come
join me by the window

and when the rosy glow of dawn
casts shadows behind us and
promise ahead, we will turn
to face each other in the light
of the new world, and my reflection
will be, always, you.

Love Letter from One Side of the Door to the Other

This is what all our conflicts boil down to:
We never are on the same side of things.
Whatever you do, I want to undo.
Some days it seems we're joined by a mere hinge.

Then there are the times when you're closed up tight,
And all I want to do is see inside.
There are times all it seems we do is fight,
But with you, I feel I don't have to hide.

We see and respect each other's own truths.
After all, we are two sides of one love.
Some folks may judge and think it is uncouth,
But I like knowing just what we're made of.

I take such great comfort in you and me,
With love as solid as mahogany.

Love Letter from a Scented Candle to a Gentle Breeze

They told me that you were bad news,
not right for me, unworthy of my trust,
but from the moment I chose you
I believed in the possibility of us.

And even when I felt low and burnt-out,
you came and held me with that comforting touch.
With your gentle nature, you helped erase my doubts
and reassured the possibility of us.

With the bravado of a tornado,
we were swept away in love.
With the intensity of an inferno,
we sparked the possibility of us.

Love is like that, but it's okay to be afraid—
impermanence is the fragrance of our days.

Love Letter from the Sunlight to the Curtains

Do you like the way I chase you around,
from dawn till dusk? You must. Even at night,
when we are miles apart, separated by stars
and windowsills, I hold you in my heart
while you hold still in the dark.

All I want now is to allow
my rays of light to rest
gently against you without
putting up a fight. And yet you
stay shut against the world,
and no beast or animal or girl

could crack you open. You mope
in darkness and you like it that way. I don't know
why I want to bathe you in the warmth
of my love anyway, but you invite me back
every day. Every day, I love you
anyway.

Do you like the way I chase you around,
from dawn till dusk, do you like the way
my very air seems to glitter
even if it's only dust?

Sestinas & Sonnets & Villanelles

Love That Dog: A Sestina

For Zeena

For years, my siblings and I had tried
to persuade my parents to let us get a dog.
I told them I needed something
to teach me responsibility, something sweet
to take care of. Something to love.
For the longest time, all they said was, "Maybe."

And for the longest time, that "maybe"
was all I had to hold on to. They tried
to satiate my need with a goldfish, but really, how can you love
a goldfish? It died two days later anyway. No, I needed a dog.
A companion. A playful, sweet
pup to be my something.

We went for a drive one day, "just for fun." But there was something
about the way Mom said it, I dared to hope that maybe
today would be the day. Sweet
anticipation… we arrived at: "Westport Humane Society – Adopt
        Today!" I tried
to contain my excitement. We walked past a dozen cages, every dog
barking relentlessly as if to say, "Me, me, pick me to love!"

And that's when we saw her, slumped in the corner of her cage, the
        sad-eyed brown dog. Love
at first sight. There was just something
about her. So we brought her home. Our new dog.

She was so timid at first, like maybe
love was not something she knew in her past life. So we tried
our best to make her happy. Our girl, so gentle and sweet.

I loved everything about her: the clicking of her nails on the kitchen
        linoleum, the sweet
way her ears perked up at the word "outside," her unconditional love.
A brand-new connection. And even if I had tried,
I knew beyond a doubt that there was just something
familiar in her that I could never replace. She was maybe
the purest animal I ever knew. I loved that dog.

For five incredible years, I loved that dog.
She had the softest fur I'd ever felt, like the petals of a sweet
flower, an entire bouquet, maybe
given to you by someone you love.
Then one day, it was clear that something
was wrong. She was shaking, so we brought her to the vet and they tried

to help my gentle, trembling dog, but sometimes there is just not
        enough love.
Now, years later, I still wonder if the bittersweet feeling of loving and
        losing something
so precious makes us love more fiercely, or maybe just more cautiously.
        I don't know. I am still trying.

Still Resonating: A Sestina

No matter where you and I went in the pursuit of sound, we
        always loved
live music, all those concerts where we lost
ourselves to the dissonance of harsh beats pulsing in time
to smooth keyboard riffs, the complex melody echoing in our heads
        long past
the much-cheered-for encore, those last
notes of an anthem we swore we'd never forget.

In a crowd full of faces I would inevitably forget,
yours was the one I fell in love
with. Before the night ended, we'd dance till the very last
song, always getting lost
in each other, getting stuck in the past,
counting our lucky stars, not the hours passed bedtime.

And I swear, every time
I looked in your eyes, it was like I'd forget
the possibility of becoming your past,
of leaving behind that kind of love.
There is nothing quite like the loss
of something we always thought would last.

We showed up for those shows, because as long as they lasted,
all that collective jiving and grooving, we had time,
we had potential before we lost

it all to differences and distance, before we forgot
the simple things, intricate nuances our love
encompassed—together, we danced as the moments passed.

But when the dancing was past,
the most resonant songs couldn't last.
Sometimes even music can't save the greatest of loves
when someone's heart beats out of time.
I never wanted to know the things you forget
when a certain kind of rhythm is lost,

but it's almost funny, how many songs I lost
to our ruined, discordant past.
Let me ask: When it's all or nothing, can a feeling be forgotten?
After so much syncopation, the very last
thing I thought I'd lose is time,
those years wasted on the wrong love.

Not quite lost but never meant to last,
the past freezes our music in time,
echoing even as I forget our half-sighed, half-sung love.

January: A Sonnet

When cumulus clouds gray as ash roll up
the wind makes haste outside my window here.
The kettle boils, I pour the jasmine cup.
It's been a long year. And so has last year.

The clouds roll by, heavy and gray as stone.
Sleepless hours pass. I think, "No more tea."
When dreams do come, I'm outside all alone
and let the freezing rain roll right off me.

I don't know what is happening in town.
Good news could come, and I'd put up a fight.
Hard to know what's real when chaos abounds.
This really can't turn out well, but it might.

I lay in bed and watch the rolling clouds.
The sky is ashen gray. The wind is loud.

Gargoyle In My Heart: A Sonnet

There's a lonely gargoyle in my heart
who creeps and lurks and watches come what may
and when my heart is shaken, torn apart
he always knows exactly what to say.

My gargoyle is my brave protector here.
When sunshine lights upon my heart, he smiles
and when things become murky and unclear,
his fearsome wail reverberates for miles.

My lonesome gargoyle is always with me—
he cannot leave even if he wanted.
With my gargoyle's love, I'm never lonely.
He keeps me safe and guarded and haunted.

He champions my heart with bold wings spread—
even if he is only in my head.

Treading Water: A Villanelle

I'm underwater, trying to escape
this invisible tide pulling me down deep—
or is it just a feeling I can't shake?

That cruel irony that won't fade away—
a mermaid strangled by her own seaweed,
underwater, but trying to escape.

Struggling with a curse I've got to break,
I resign myself to treading water—
or is it just a feeling I can't shake?

Above my muddled head, the waves murmur—
it's hard to see if things are what they seem
while underwater, trying to escape.

I can't face it myself, there's too much space
and too much distance for a clear picture
of this murky feeling I just can't shake.

Can't even tell if it will fade or stay
or maybe keep pressing down so I can't breathe.
I'm underwater, trying to escape
whatever this feeling is that I can't shake.

Another Mad Girl's Love Song: A Villanelle

And so it goes, another love gone dead;
I fear another will not bloom again.
(I still hear your music inside my head.)

I used to dress up all in lively red,
but love's cruel dim clouds came rolling in.
And so it goes, another love gone dead.

I think of you when I lay down to bed;
my moon-lit dreams drive me near-half insane.
(I still hear your music inside my head.)

The clocks tick on, but memories won't fade;
you are no longer more than other men.
And so it goes, another love gone dead.

"You will marry a music man," they said,
but time has passed since you last spoke my name.
(I still hear your music inside my head.)

Some days I wish I'd been born deaf instead;
at least I'd never hear the past again.
And so it goes, another love gone dead.
(I still hear your music inside my head.)

Et Cetera

Storytelling

All the birds migrating now;
The great Vs of geese hasten and pause.
They build lovely and sometimes perfect music,
A familiar whistleable melody,
storytelling.
So euphoric that you can hear the depressing ending before it comes.

They are singing a love unrequited,
quite possibly unacknowledged.
They're so common, always in plain sight,
flying low; just out of reach above us,
sometimes we overlook them.

The great Vs of geese hasten and pause,
all the birds migrating now.

Step One

Flawless like air –

      right?

But I am miles from unseeing burned-in memories.
In the beginning of cobbling together the past,

I'm here,

      hitting twenty-eight shades of one heart,

      struggling with escaping details,

      screaming questions through a poem.

I don't know how to make up a deep conviction to change.

But context first—
my story is a longtime dream

      to figure out,

      take seriously,

      get right.

I want my behind-the-scenes confidence
to seep through everything.

Looking back, I see it—

the dark-rimmed turbulence,
a bright
          everlasting
                    swan-dive
                              into
                                    authenticity.

Dusk

Way past afternoon,
the sky tips,
plunging into the realm beyond.

Panoramic views of the sky
dazzle the world with rolling clouds,
electric lights, and delicate marvels.

This eclectic parade of colors
swirls dizzyingly,
a peaceful expanse of airspace.

Then comes evening, a more somber air
where the sun is quick
to collapse and disappear.

In the dark,
the solar kaleidoscope changes,
graceful and illuminated.

The surface is set mirror-still
filled with the stellar glow of stars,
unified oneness.

Even clear-eyed time
can't help but blink
at the joy found there.

The Moon Made Me Do It

Don't worry about
that letter I sent you.
The one about
my previously undisclosed
feelings for you.

The moon made me do it.

In my defense,
the new Taylor Swift album
had just come out

and it was 2 a.m.
My curtains were open
so I could look at the trees

and the moon was there,
a luminous wink.
She said *truth or dare*
and I chose both.

Recessive

Consider the delicate probability
of Punnett squares—
those big Bs and little bs,
handing out dominant browns,
gifting recessive blues.

Consider the wild improbability
of knowledgeable stares—
when brown and blue eyes meet,
a love connection crowns
generations of optical hues.

Consider the earnest fragility
behind every chromosome pair—
the dominant genes
pushing recessive down,
and they hardly ever lose.

Consider the fierce agility
of my dad's genes that dared
to defy convention and gave me
eyes so blue that they wowed
Mother Nature against her own rules.

Communication

The glow of the moon spotlights clear views of the mountain
  though they never touch.

The shade of the trees inspires grassy fields to grow
  though it rarely observes this detail.

The shore does not feel the full depth of the lake
  though it is a marvelous sight.

I stand at the edge of this sprawling distance and know
  we do not need words to connect.

In the shuffle of river and moonlight
  an unimagined bridge holds shared potential—

But we dare not cross it, for fear of the water
  rushing, overwhelming, shimmering.

Let's Make a Deal

When I think about telling you,
I think about the choice.
Risk versus reward.

Behind door number one:

a pitying shake of the head, eyes averted,
the clock running out as a buzzer sounds,

a mumbled rejection disguised
as a polite excuse, probably something
about friendship,

the realization I read too much into
things, wanted too much, wanted it
too badly,

wanted you

when you were elsewhere
the whole time,

a balloon drop of disappointment as
the lights dim.

I win a blender and puree my own heart,
ever the willing contestant.

Behind door number two:

you next to me,
sudden proximity like a spotlight, my
heart buzzes and the audience cheers,

relief and jubilation like cymbals crashing,
all the right answers to all the right questions,

finally, finally, finally,
you and me in lights.

I win a luxury car and we drive
off into the sunset.

Behind door number three:

a dark closet that I stuff my heart into,
slamming the door and tossing the key,

a future, albeit a casual one,
true affection sprinkled throughout
occasional encounters, perhaps for years,

a picture frame of two friends,
gathering dust, hanging in the balance,
hanging in there.

I wanted a loveseat and I win a lawn chair.

When I think about telling you,
I think about the choice.
Risk versus reward.

This game has rules that I don't understand
and I've never been very lucky,

but you make me want to win.

Maps

Lately I've been looking for something.
Compass in hand, I meander around my mind, that vast
inner vault of decisions and flaws.

The gardens of a lush yet prickly psyche bloom
with forget-me-nots and vines. I observe
wits drifting swiftly on the wind and occasionally trip
over stray intrusive thoughts, popping up like rooted knots
around steadfast trees of stolid beliefs. Passing by
a vast ocean of subconscious motives, I take a breath
and marvel at the soft waves of dreams tangled up in seaweed.

Located at the corner of charmingly boring and halfway indifferent,
my low-key persona is a small neighborhood that welcomes few—
the library is old, but the tavern is new.

I have half a mind to romp around the playground
of childhood, innocent, safe, carefree, but it's off-limits,
tucked away in the historic district of memory where
light streams through mosaic windows and the air is always clean.

I try to explore the skyscraper of adulthood, the sensibilities
and sought-after stability within, but it's still under construction, skeletal
steel beams
extending into an impossible, ever-shifting future. I just can't
see it yet, even when I step back and crane my neck.

So I return to my multi-bedroom imagination,
the closets stuffed with stories and secrets.
Reflecting in the mirror of my mind's eye, I realize I want
to knock on someone's door and find their kitchen light on,
the kettle on the stove and the warm glow of an unfamiliar yet
welcoming home.
For all the sprawling gardens and half-made buildings in my head,
I really want to build a bridge.

We'll sit and spread our maps out on the dining table, breathing close
as we read them and taking notes for love—light gray pencil marks
and subtle sparks—careful blueprints, an imagined us.

Cursive

When I was a child,
my grandmother demonstrated
how to write my name in cursive
on a small slip
of cream-colored paper.

I loved the way it looked—
all those loopy letters,

each character connected,
every sentence a family,

blurring into one another,
holding hands crossing the street.

Eventually I learned how to write
in cursive,
whole paragraphs if necessary.
My name.

Some of the letters
I could never remember,
so I made them up as I went.

They always told me
the point of cursive
was to save time
by never having to pick up
your pen.

I always thought
cursive
took
extra
time

but they said
I was still learning.

My mom writes in excellent cursive.
My grandmother did too.
Auntie.
Nana.
All the women in my family knew
exquisite cursive.

When I got to school, they nearly stopped
teaching it.
But I practiced.

Years passed.

The women who celebrated the birth
of my sister and me
passed away.

No one writes in cursive much
these days.

I think
I am still learning.

Acknowledgments

First, I am so grateful to everyone who read, purchased, hyped up, and/or believed in this little book. It's been a long time coming, but we made it.

Many thanks to my family, for always supporting my writing endeavors and (usually) not minding having a temperamental poet in the family. You're all amazing, and I'm so lucky.

Thanks especially to my twin sister Cait, who is my biggest champion as well as my favorite person. Love you CJ.

Big shout-out to Mary Oliver, for writing a poem about geese that got stuck in my brain once and influenced everything I did from there on out.

Thank you to all of my wonderful English teachers and writing professors over the years for their indelible instruction and encouragement.

Last but not least, thank you to Dani Dymond for her thoughtful and insightful help in preparing this manuscript. As your name suggests, you indeed shine.